AN EASY-READ FACT BOOK

Tanks

Michael Jay

Franklin Watts

London New York Sydney Toronto

The picture on the previous page shows an M-1 Abrams tank. It is waiting to ambush an "enemy" in practice maneuvers.

© 1987 Franklin Watts
First published in Great Britain 1987 by
Franklin Watts
12a Golden Square
London W1

First published in the USA by
Franklin Watts Inc.
387 Park Avenue South
New York
N.Y. 10016

UK ISBN 0 86313 496 3
US ISBN 0-531-10279-3
Library of Congress Catalog
Card Number: 86-50637

Designed by
David Jefferis/Sunrise Books

Illustrated by
Drawing Attention
Robert Burns
Hayward Art Group
Michael Roffe

Photographs supplied by
AAI Corporation
Hughes Aircraft Co.
Military Archive and
Research Services
A. Moore
Swedish Army
M. Tricks
US Air Force
US Army

Technical consultant
Andrew McNeil

AN
EASY-READ
FACT
BOOK

Tanks

Contents

Heavyweight warrior

This heavily armored machine is a typical modern tank. The big gun turret swivels around, so that the main gun can fire in any direction.

For night fighting, tanks have searchlights and low–light TV cameras. Detectors can spot sources of heat, such as soldiers or other tanks, even in pitch darkness.

Most tanks have diesel engines, which are reliable and powerful.

▽ This 40mt (44 ton) tank is armed with a big main gun, a smaller cannon and a machine gun. A smoke system can inject diesel fuel into the engine exhaust. This creates a dense black cloud to hide the tank.

Cannon

Main gun

Low-light TV camera provides vision at night. Its view is shown on a screen inside the turret.

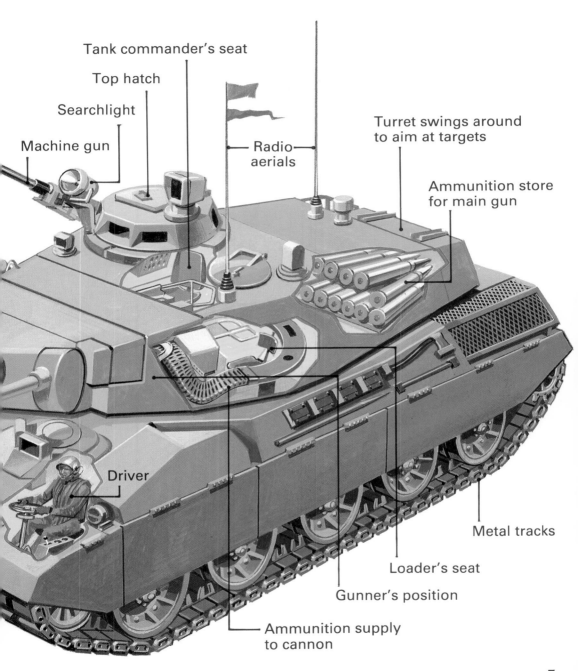

Tank commander's seat

Top hatch

Searchlight

Machine gun

Radio aerials

Turret swings around to aim at targets

Ammunition store for main gun

Driver

Metal tracks

Loader's seat

Gunner's position

Ammunition supply to cannon

Commanding a tank

Most tanks have a crew of three or four. They climb in through hatches.

The commander is in charge. He can stand up, with his head and shoulders out of the top hatch, to direct operations. In a battle, the hatch is shut and the commander looks out through all-round-view periscopes. For night fighting, sensitive TV cameras can be used. "Starlight scopes" pick up even

▽ An M-1 Abrams tank displays its unusual angled turret. Commander and crew can quickly seal themselves in when necessary.

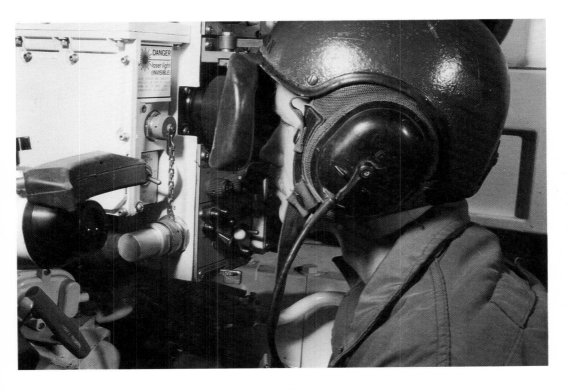

the faintest light. An electronic image is shown on a TV screen.

The driver sits toward the front. He guides the tank with two steering levers, accelerator and gearbox. To turn the tank, the tracks on one side are slowed or stopped. The tank swings around, driven by the other tracks.

The gunner aims and fires the main gun. Some tanks have automatic loading systems, but most have a fourth crewman who loads the gun.

△ An M-1 gunner takes careful aim. A laser beam is used to track targets.

Aiming and firing

In the heat of battle, hitting a distant target is not easy. To help, modern tanks have computers.

The commander decides on the target and orders the gunner to take aim. The gunner pinpoints the enemy in his sights. The tank computer then shifts the aiming spot, making adjustments to allow for movement and the target distance. It also allows for wind direction – a strong wind can blow a shell off-course. The gunner checks that the target is dead center. Then he is ready to fire.

1

Gun stays at same
angle to keep on target.

△ The sequence above
shows how a tank gun
can keep on target,
even when moving on
rough ground. The gun

barrel swings up and
down to adjust for the
changing angle of the
tank.

◁ Here you can see
how computers help to
track a target.
1 Commander selects
target. Gunner puts
aiming spot on it.
2 Computer works out
range, allowing for
wind and tank's motion.
3 Computer shifts
aiming mark (the red
oval shape).
4 Gunner moves sights
so target is in aiming
oval and ... fires!

2   **3**   **4**

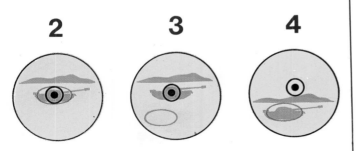

Shells and armor

▽Reactive armor is a recent development.
1 Shell or missile is fired at tank.
2 As shell starts to penetrate, armor explodes outward, destroying the shell.
3 The Bill missile is made to get through reactive armor. It blows a powerful jet-blast through the armor and into the tank below.

Tanks can fire various types of shell. Squash–head shells flatten on impact, sending a shockwave through armor plate. Armor-piercing shells are made to punch a hole through armor. Tanks can carry a combination of these and other types of shell.

Armor plate is as thick as possible. But if armor is *too* thick, a tank becomes heavy and slow, making itself

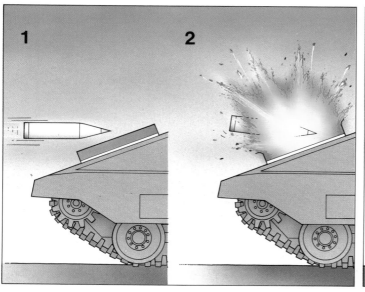

a sitting duck for enemy guns.

Reactive armor can be laid on top of normal armor. When hit by a shell or missile, reactive armor explodes outward, destroying the incoming projectile with its own force.

There are ways to get through reactive armor, though. The Swedish "Bill" missile is designed to explode in a jet of flame, strong enough to blast straight through reactive armor and the tank's own metal cladding.

△ "S" tanks like this have no turret. They rely on the suspension to move the gun up and down. The tracks swing the gun from side to side.

These tanks have bulldozer blades to dig defensive positions in the ground. The tanks then lie in wait for the enemy.

On the western front

▽ These Mk IV tanks could go through barbed wire entanglements. This was impossible for soldiers without spending dangerous minutes cutting the wire. Tanks sometimes carried bundles of fascines. These were piles of wood which could be dropped into a wide trench or ditch. The tank could then easily cross the gap.

Tanks were first developed during World War I. The war was at a stalemate on the western front. The flat landscape of the front ran through northern France and part of Belgium. Soldiers, hidden in trenches, made advances by either side almost impossible.

The armored tank changed the situation. In 1917, 476 British tanks were sent into action at Cambrai. They punched a hole through the German

defenses of over 3 km (2 miles), an amazing distance at the time. These early tanks were slow and awkward – Mark IV tanks trundled along at less than 6 km/h (4 mph).

The first French tanks were the Schneider and St. Chamonds, introduced in 1917. The only German tank in the war was the 18-man A7V.

△ Inside a World War I tank.
1 Metal tracks.
2 Fuel tank.
3 Ammunition supply.
4 Driver.

Blitzkrieg

△ This color photograph shows troops advancing with a PzKpfw III tank. This tank had a very powerful gun, designed to disable other tanks.

"Panzer" is the German word for armor. The word for tank is Panzerkampf-wagen, which means armored battle vehicle.

Blitzkrieg means "lightning war" and it was used in World War II. German armies used men and machines to cut speedily through enemy lines.

Phase One of Blitzkrieg used armored cars and motorcycles to check out enemy positions. Meanwhile, dive bombers created havoc among enemy troops and behind the lines.

Phase Two used tanks and troops, carried in lorries and armored trucks, to attack the weaker points, taking them quickly. Points of resistance

were left to follow-up troops.

In attacks like these, tanks were not the big, heavy types, but lighter ones. These were faster and much more maneuverable.

Tanks have been used to win many battles since then.

△ Tanks supported infantry wherever necessary in Blitzkrieg attacks. Here, the streets of a Russian town fall to Panzer tank divisions.

Desert battles

△ The British Crusader III (top) and the American Sherman (bottom) did much desert fighting. The Sherman was built in huge numbers – about 49,000 were made during World War II.

The tanks shown above were all used in desert battles. These were fought on the sands of North Africa, in the early part of World War II.

It became clear that whoever had the best tanks would win the desert war. Guns, speed and armor improved. Early designs, such as the Italian M13/40, had a 47mm caliber gun. Later types, such as the M-4 Sherman, had 75mm guns.

Caliber describes the width across the inside of a gun barrel. The bigger it is, the bigger the round of ammunition that can be fired. Tanks like the present–day Abrams have massive 120mm guns. Size is not the only factor in gun design, though. For example, high muzzle velocity – the speed at which a shell leaves the barrel – helps the shell punch through armor better than a slower shot.

△ Italian tanks included the 14 mt (15.4 ton) M-14/40 (top). German tanks included the fast and heavily armed PzKpfw IV (bottom).

Modern tanks

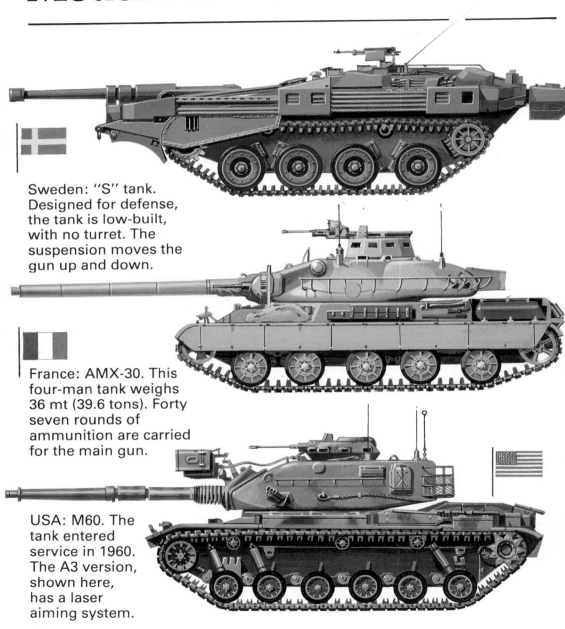

Sweden: "S" tank. Designed for defense, the tank is low-built, with no turret. The suspension moves the gun up and down.

France: AMX-30. This four-man tank weighs 36 mt (39.6 tons). Forty seven rounds of ammunition are carried for the main gun.

USA: M60. The tank entered service in 1960. The A3 version, shown here, has a laser aiming system.

Britain: Chieftain. A four-man tank, weighing 55 mt (60.5 tons). Its gun is very powerful and has an accurate range of over 2,010 m (2,200 yards).

West Germany: Leopard 2. This tank has advanced armor and a snorkel system for the engine, so the Leopard can ford deep rivers.

USSR: T-72. Has long-range fuel tanks, carried at the rear. The side-skirt boxes are thought to hold anti missile armor.

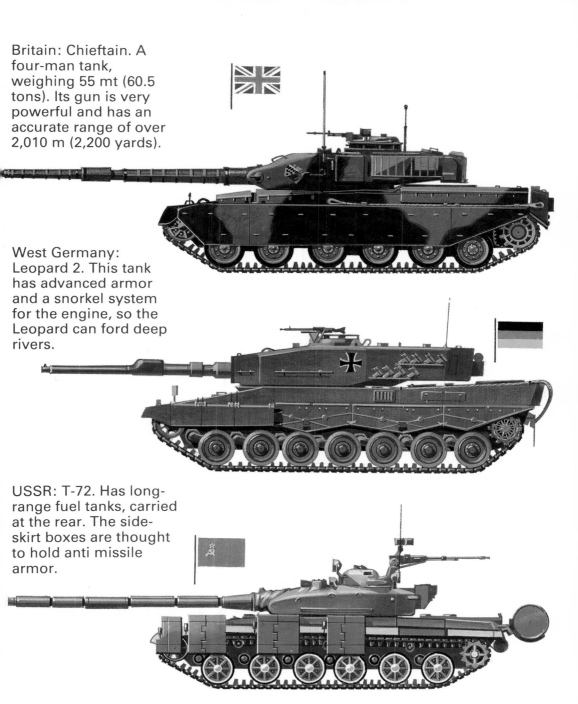

On exercise

△ Tank crews take a breather during Exercise Lionheart. The tanks are British Challengers, camouflaged to blend in with the landscape of northern Europe.

If a war breaks out, there is unlikely to be any time to practice before the fighting starts. Therefore, drill is very important for all military forces.

Military exercises can be small- or large-scale. Sometimes, ground, air and sea forces are used. Forces are split in two. One side defends, the other attacks. Umpires check the success and failures of the two sides.

Training areas in remote places can be used. But for really big exercises, tanks and troops may have to go over plowed fields and public highways. Compensation is paid to civilians such as farmers, whose crops may have been damaged.

Some live weapons are fired, but most are blanks. The umpires decide if a "hit" has been achieved.

△ Turrets swung sideways. These M-60A3 tanks of the US Army take careful aim during firing practice.

Tank killers

The tank has ruled the battlefield for 70 years, but its days may be numbered. Modern missiles make a tank an easy target to destroy.

There are many lightweight anti tank missiles which can be carried by soldiers. Troops can stay hidden with their portable missile launchers, waiting for a tank to come in range. Once fired, a missile is almost unstoppable.

Even more dangerous are missile-firing helicopter gunships. These can hover behind trees, pop up for a few seconds to fire missiles and then dive back under cover again. Recent battles have seen as many as 48 tanks destroyed for every chopper shot down.

The A-10 anti tank plane has a massive gun under its nose. The gun can fire at a rate of over 4,000 rounds per minute. The shells can smash through the toughest tank armor.

▷ This unusual view of a "tank-busting" A-10 shows off its gun well. You can see the weapon, poking out, just below the plane's nose.

The A-10 carries bombs and missiles too.

▷ The Milan anti tank missile is used by several armies. Each missile is kept in its own sealed tube. After launching the missile, the soldier simply keeps the target in his sights to get a hit.

Tank of the future

The tank of the future will be very different from the large and bulky machines of today.

The design shown on these pages could be the look of tomorrow's tank. It is much smaller than present-day

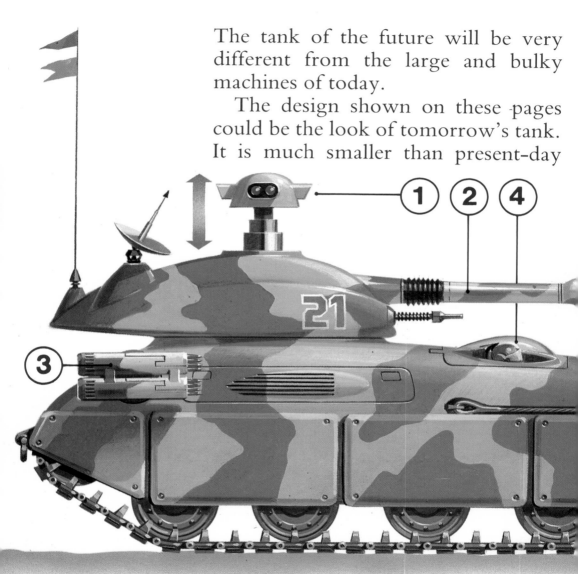

machines, which makes it a difficult target to aim at.

The small size and weight means that it can go fast as well – anything up to 100 km/h (62 mph) through rough country. Specially designed armor deflects missiles and shells. The crew is reduced to just two, commander-gunner and driver, with lots of help from computers.

▽ Key to future tank.
1 Periscope has various sensors for day and night fighting.
2 Gun fires shells and missiles.
3 Anti aircraft missiles knock out planes and helicopter gunships.
4 Driver's position. Tank carries a crew of two. Gunloading is automatic.
5 Armor.

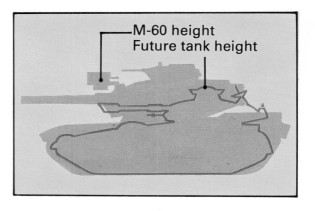

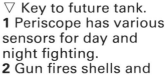

M-60 height
Future tank height

Special tanks

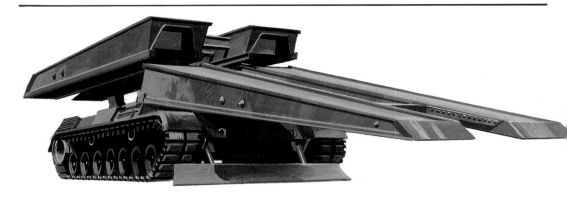

There have been lots of strange looking tanks, made for special work on the battlefield.

The 1944 bobbin, or carpet, tank carried a big roll of tough canvas. The tank unwound the roll and laid a canvas track on soft ground. Other tanks could use the track to cross the soft ground safely.

Flail tanks beat a path through mine-fields. The metal flails spun around, setting off mines in front of the advancing tank. This made a safe, mine-free path, which other tanks could follow.

Modern special tanks function as cranes, drills and bridge layers.

△▽ The German Leopard comes in various models. Above, a bridge-layer carries a "Scissors" bridge, which unfolds to cross small rivers. Below, a crane-auger can drill holes several feet deep.

◁ This bobbin, or carpet, tank was used in World War II. It carried 91 m (100 yards) of canvas track. This unrolled to let the tank cross soft ground, such as sandy beaches.

▷ Another World War II design, this tank had spinning metal flails. These set off any mines laid in front of the tank. Some modern tanks are equipped with heavy bulldozer blades to achieve the same thing.

70 years of tanks

These pictures give you some idea of the way tanks have changed since the earliest machines of World War I.

△ Artist and inventor Leonardo da Vinci made sketches of tank-like machines in the 15th century.

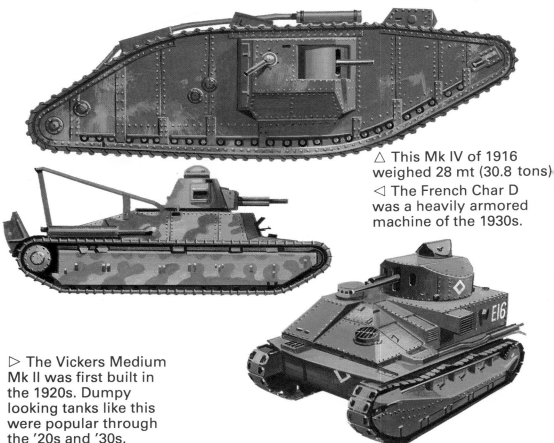

△ This Mk IV of 1916 weighed 28 mt (30.8 tons)

◁ The French Char D was a heavily armored machine of the 1930s.

▷ The Vickers Medium Mk II was first built in the 1920s. Dumpy looking tanks like this were popular through the '20s and '30s.

28

◁ The Russian T34 of 1941 mounted a powerful gun and had thick, sloping armor. Its cross-country speed was over 50 km/h (31 mph).

▷ The Tiger 1E was one of many German designs in World War II.

▽ The British Centurion was a successful tank of the 1950s.

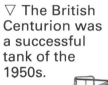

◁ The T62 was a 1960s Russian design. This one has extra fuel drums at the back for long range patrols.

Glossary

Here are some of the technical words used in this book.

Armor
The tough metal which protects a tank.
Armor can be made of various materials. A typical metal is toughened nickel-chrome alloy steel. The thickness of armor varies – that of a Chieftain tank reaches a maximum of 152 mm (6 inches) on the front decking.
Some modern armor is made in multiple layers. This helps absorb hits more effectively.

Blitzkrieg
The word is pronounced BLITZ-KREEG, and is German for "lightning war."
It was used to describe the swift armored attacks used in the early stages of World War II.

Caliber
The inside diameter of a gun barrel. The British Chieftain tank has a very powerful 120mm-caliber gun.

Camouflage
Paint scheme to hide a tank against its ground. In desert warfare, tanks are painted sandy brown. In northern Europe, camouflage of brown and green is used. In winter conditions, white is often used.

Gunship
Type of helicopter, armed with powerful gun and missile armament. The latest types have periscope sights mounted above the rotor. With these they can hover behind trees, then pop up to fire missiles.

Laser
Powerful beam of light, used by many modern tanks as a rangefinder and aiming device.

Muzzle
The open end of a gun.

Shell
Type of ammunition fired by a tank. Shells can be HE (high explosive) or AP (armor piercing). HE squash-heads flatten on impact, then explode, sending a shockwave through armor. AP shells are more accurate at long range.

Snorkel
Breathing tube which enables an engine to work underwater. It supplies air, necessary for any engine.

Suspension
The system of wheels, coils and springs which enables a tank to travel over rough country at high speed.

Trench
Deep, straight-sided ditch dug to provide protection for troops. Used especially in World War I.

Tank facts

De Mole's landship
In 1912, an inventor called De Mole suggested a "landship" design. It was armored and had metal tracks. Later tanks were very similar to his concept.

Secret code name
How did a large armored vehicle come to be called a tank? When the first machines were secretly being developed, they were given a code name to avoid giving spies an idea of what was going on. The code name was "water tank"!

Males and females
Mark IV tanks were made in two types, "male" and "female." Males had heavy guns, females had several machine guns.

The first tank-against-tank battle was at Villers-Bretonneux, in France. Here, on April 24th 1918, British Mk IVs fought German A7Vs.

△ Officers and men of the Canadian army get a ride aboard a Mark IV tank. The photograph was taken in June 1918, five months before the end of World War I.

The biggest tank battle
At Kursk in 1943, over 6,000 tanks of the German and Russian armies fought the biggest tank battle ever.

Heaviest tank
This was a German machine, the "Maus II." It weighed 188 mt (206.8 tons)!

Index